918.1

Global Cities
RIO DE JANEIRO

Simon Scoones
Photographs by Edward Parker

Evans

Published by
Evans Brothers Limited,
Part of the Evans Publishing Group,
2A Portman Mansions
Chiltern Street
London WIU 6NR

First published 2006

British Library Cataloguing in Publication Data

Scoones, Simon
Rio de Janeiro. - (Global cities)
I.Rio de Janeiro (Brazil) - Juvenile literature
I.Title
981.5'3065

ISBN-10: 023753102X
13-digit ISBN (from I January 2007) 9780237 531 027

Designer: Robert Walster, Big Blu Design
Maps and graphics by Martin Darlinson
All photographs are by Edward Parker except
Corbis 12b, 48b, 49t
Viviane Moos/Corbis 22b

Series concept and project management EASI –
Educational Resourcing
(info@easi-er.co.uk)

Contents

Living in an urban world

Sometime in 2007 the world's population will, for the first time, become more urban than rural. An estimated 3.3 billion people will find themselves living in towns and cities like Rio, and for many, the experience of urban living will be relatively new. In China, the world's most populous country, the number of people living in urban areas increased from 196 million in 1980 to over 536 million by 2005.

The urban challenge...

This staggering rate of urbanisation (the process by which a country's population becomes concentrated into towns and cities), is being repeated across much of the world and presents the world with a complex set of challenges for the twenty-first century. Many of these challenges are local, like the provision of clean water for expanding urban populations, but others are global in scale. In 2003 an outbreak of the highly contagious SARS disease demonstrated this as it spread rapidly among the populations of well-connected cities across the globe. The pollution generated by urban areas is also a global concern, particularly as urban residents tend to generate more than their rural counterparts.

▼ Rio de Janeiro in relation to the rest of Brazil and its neighbouring countries (inset) and its immediate surrounding area.

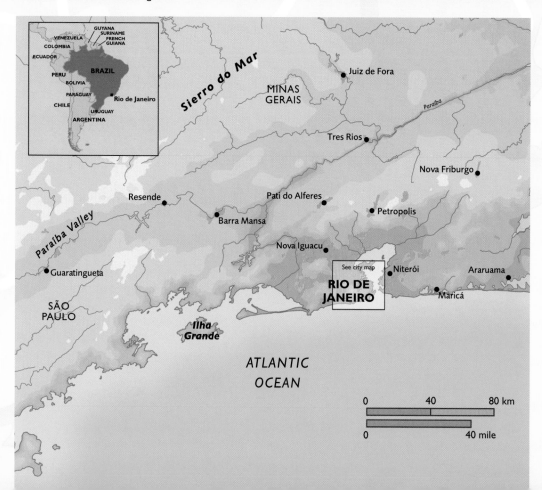

... and opportunity!

Urban centres and particularly major cities like Rio de Janeiro also provide great opportunities for improving life at both a local and global scale. Cities concentrate people and allow for efficient forms of mass transport like subway or light rail networks. Services too, such as waste collection, recycling, education and health can all function more efficiently in a city.

Cities are also centres of learning, and often the birthplace of new ideas, from innovations in science and technology to new ways of day-to-day living. Cities provide a platform for the celebration of arts and culture too. As their populations become more multicultural such celebrations are increasingly global in their origins and reach.

▲ The most exclusive parts of Rio are clustered around Guanabara Bay, with its views of Sugar Loaf Mountain.

A global city

Although all urban centres share certain things in common there are a number of cities in which the challenges and opportunities facing an urban world are particularly concentrated. These can be thought of as 'global cities' – cities that in themselves provide a window on the wider world and reflect the challenges of urbanisation, of globalisation, of citizenship and of sustainable development, that face us all.

Rio de Janeiro is one such global city. With over 11 million inhabitants (locally known as *cariocas*), Rio is the 14th most populated city in the world. Yet many argue that Rio has an even greater influence and presence on the world stage. During Brazil's 300 years as Portugal's biggest and most important colony, Rio was the capital city of the country. In 1960, Brasilia replaced Rio as Brazil's capital but many Brazilians still regard Rio as the centre of Brazilian life. What's more, people around the world marvel at Rio's spectacular setting, overlooking Guanabara Bay and hemmed in by steep mountains. This book introduces you to the city and its people and investigates just what makes Rio de Janeiro a truly 'global city'.

The marvellous city

The people of Rio de Janeiro call their city, the *cidade maravilhosa*, the marvellous city. As well as its stunning scenery, each February, Rio hosts one of the world's biggest parties, known as Carnival. For five days and nights, cariocas join visitors from all over the world to take part in colourful parades, and dance to the sounds of samba and bossa nova rhythms that were born in Rio. The city's beaches, like Copacabana and Ipanema, are the destinations for millions of tourists. Rio is also the birthplace of some of the greatest soccer stars, and boasts the world's largest football stadium, the Maracanã, named after the local river running through the district. Away from the beaches and nightclubs, the city can present a very different face, with poor conditions is some *favelas* (shanty towns) that cling to the hillsides, and which are the home to millions of residents.

▼ The centre of Rio de Janeiro.

A view from Sugar Loaf

One of the most striking aspects of Rio is its setting amidst mountains or *serra* that are part of the Sierra do Mar mountain range. The steep slopes of the serra are made of granite that have withstood millions of years of erosion by wind and water. Soaring 394 m above the heart of the city is Sugar Loaf mountain. The Portuguese christened it, 'Sugar Loaf' as they thought it looked like the moulds that were used to set sugar cane. Today, both residents and tourists can take a cable car to the summit to take in (or marvel at) the breathaking views.

Rio began as a Portuguese settlement situated on one of the serra called Morro de Castelo. Like many other hills in the city, Morro de Castelo was later flattened and the debris was used to fill in swampy

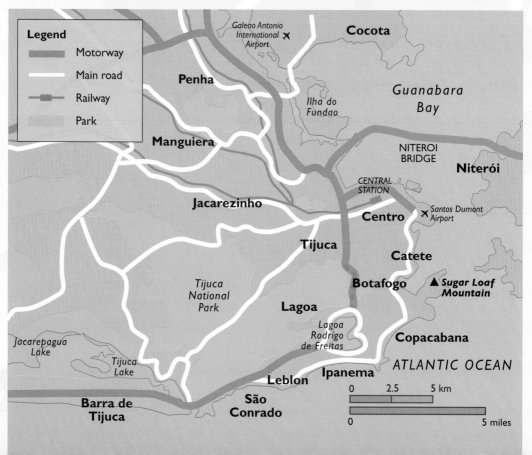

▲ Cable cars take tourists to the top of the Sugar Loaf for a view across the city.

lowland to make room for more buildings. Gradually the city grew, and some of Guanabara Bay was also filled in and turned into new land. Neighbourhoods sprang up between the hills and mountains, and the serra effectively divided the city into two halves. North of the serra the area known as *zona norte* was flatter and easier to build on. Further south, the narrow strip of land squeezed between the mountains and the sea called *zona sul* developed into one of the world's most densely populated areas.

Two cities

The *zona norte* is a polluted industrial region, home to poorer communities that work in the factories and in other low paid jobs. People live in housing projects, or in neighbourhoods built illegally on hillsides or in ravines. These shanty towns, or favelas, are scattered across the city. An underworld of competing drug gangs has turned some *favelas* into extremely dangerous places to live. Meanwhile, most of the richer residents live in the *zona sul*.

Along the beachfront in the *zona sul*, residents enjoy one of the most luxurious lifestyles in the world.

▼ A *favela* clinging to one of the steep hillsides.

The history of Rio

In 1494 Portugal annexed Brazil as a colony. Seven years later, three Portuguese ships under the command of Amerigo Vespucci were sent to explore Brazil's coastline. On New Year's Day 1502, they reached a narrow opening. Beyond lay a body of water that Vespucci wrongly guessed was the mouth of a river. In fact it was a beautiful bay named Guanabara (or 'arm of the sea') by the Amerindians that lived there. Vespucci called this stretch of water, 'the January river' (Rio de Janeiro in Portugese), and the name has stuck ever since.

The city was born

Despite Portugal colonising Brazil, merchants from France were the first to settle in the area. They built a fort on Seregipe Island, now part of the mainland, but the son of Brazil's third governor, Estácio de Sá, drove out the French in 1565. At the foot of Sugar Loaf mountain the victorious Estácio de Sá declared that this would be the site of a great city.

A trading hub

Rio quickly grew in the years that followed. Portuguese ships docked here to unload slaves brought over from West Africa to harvest the plantations inland. Plantation crops like sugar cane were shipped back to Europe. Gold was traded here too, thanks to a road that linked Rio to the gold mines in neighbouring Minas Gerais state. Other links inland followed age-old

▼ This farmer is planting a new crop of sugar cane. Sugar cane was one of Rio's first exports to Europe.

Amerindian routes, and ship-borne traders made more connections with other trading outposts up and down the coast. Meanwhile, ships arrived at the port loaded with cargo from Europe and elsewhere.

In 1763, the Portuguese made Rio the colonial capital of Brazil. By then, 30,000 people lived in the city, and for the next two centuries Rio went unchallenged as the country's most important city. But it also became the centre for growing resentment against the Portuguese. In 1792, a dentist called Joaquim José da Silva Xavier (nicknamed Tiradentes, or 'tooth puller') became leader of a Brazilian protest movement against Portuguese rule. Two years later, he was captured and executed on April 21 1794. In Rio his head and body parts were displayed for all to see as a warning to others against future uprisings.

After the Frenchman Napoleon Bonaparte's army invaded Portugal in 1808, the royal family fled to the safety of Rio. Although the king moved back to Portugal in 1820, his son, Dom Pedro, stayed behind. Two years later, Dom Pedro declared Brazil's independence from Portugal and became emperor. Yet this did not stop a growing wave of discontent among the population. In 1831 rioting broke out in protest at the rising cost of living. Dom Pedro could not keep the peace and after ten years he left the emperor's throne to his five-year-old son, Pedro II. Although largely a figurehead, Pedro II remained emperor of Brazil for over half a century.

From gold to coffee

During the 1800s, the mines in Minas Gerais were running out of gold, and coffee became the new trade. Coffee plantations covered the Paraíba valley, not far from the city. Coffee barons grew rich on this new crop, living in palatial mansions on the city's edge. At the same time,

railways were built that linked Rio to other places, marking the beginning of a new industrial era.

▼ As well as trade, the Portugese introduced Catholicism, now the religion of most Rio residents.

▲ Throughout the nineteenth century the construction of railway and tram lines increased the economic capacity of the city, as materials and goods passed through the city.

A new republic

When Portuguese rule finally ended in 1889, the first government of the new Republic of Brazil was based in Rio. In the Republic's early years, coffee barons and other wealthy merchants remained powerful. Many people accused them of rigging the 1930 presidential elections. A military coup followed and the runner-up in the election, a cattle rancher called Getúlio Vargas, became the new president. Vargas remained in office for the next 15 years. In an attempt to break the stranglehold of power held by the rich, Vargas became a dictator by making more decisions himself. Although he was thrown out of office by the military in 1945, Vargas was re-elected in 1950. His second term as president was dogged by corruption scandals and an economy in chaos. Hours after he was forced to resign, again by the military in 1954, Vargas shot himself in Rio's Palàcio de Catete.

Despite Brazil's turbulent early years as a republic, Rio entered a golden age in the early 1900s. Posh casinos and nightclubs opened up, and the city became a top location to make movies. Scandals became commonplace at the luxurious Copacabana Palace hotel as wealthy guests from Hollywood and the international jetset gathered to behave badly. The hotel still stands today, now restored to its former glory with its own art gallery and theatre.

Culture and trade

In 1960 the Brazilian government moved out of Rio to the new capital city of Brasilia, a newly built settlement in the centre of the country. Nevertheless, Rio remained the capital of culture and trade.
A hotel building boom took place along the city's palm-fringed beachfront, and the city developed a reputation as a centre for liberal thinkers that sought an end to the succession of military governments that ruled Brazil from 1964. With inflation spiralling out of control, citizens protested in the city's streets against the rising cost of living and the brutal violence and torture carried out by the military police.

Vast foreign debts and growing unrest finally persuaded the military generals to step aside in 1985. Despite the corruption scandals that have rocked Brazilian governments since then, the return to democracy gave people the right to replace unpopular governments. Although the cost of living continues to rise, and many live in poverty, people in modern Rio are confident the days of oppression are gone.

Football fever

During the twentieth century football became the most popular sport in Brazil. In August 1948 a suburb of Rio was chosen as the location for a brand new stadium. On July 16 1950, a record-breaking 174,000 people crammed into the Maracanã stadium to watch Brazil play Uruguay in the World Cup final. With the score at 1-1, the Uruguayan team broke the hearts of home supporters by scoring the winning goal 11 minutes from time. For two hours after the match, spectators sat in stunned silence. Brazil has since gone on to win the World Cup five times, a record unmatched by any other country, and a source of pride to its citizens.

▼ Despite an uncertain economic climate Rio, helped by its status as a major port, continued to expand throughout the second half of the twentieth century.

The people of Rio

The name cariocas given to residents of Rio originally came from the Tupi-Guaraní Amerindians as a name for a white person's house. At this time, Amerindians lived separately from their European invaders.

A multicultural city

Today, most city dwellers are mixed race. Regardless of their background, cariocas proudly celebrate the many aspects of Rio's culture that originate from their variety of ancestors. Some have ancestors who were slaves shipped over from West Africa during colonial times. Many others can trace their family roots back to Portugal, whilst some are descendants of other European migrants from Britain, France, Germany and Italy. Other people moved to Rio from Lebanon and there are some residents with Japanese ancestry.

▶ Few city dwellers are descended from a single ethnic background.

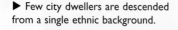

CASE STUDY

Sigrid, Botanical Gardens resident

Sigrid moved to Rio from South Africa with her husband, Gustav, 25 years ago. Gustav is a mining engineer and supplies equipment to mines across Brazil. To begin with, they lived in Ipanema, close to the beach. In those days, Ipanema was a relaxed place and they swam in the sea every day. In 2000 Sigrid and Gustav moved out because the area had become too crowded and crime levels were on the rise. Also, the beach and sea had become polluted. They now live close to the Botanical Gardens. For them, this neighbourhood feels much safer. It is only possible to enter their housing complex by showing ID to a guard on one of the gated entrances.

A multi-faith city

During colonial times, the Portuguese insisted that Catholicism was the only acceptable religion. Although today residents can practise any religion they like, most of them are still Catholic. Many actively practising Catholics living in modern Rio take a more liberal view of their faith. For example, contraceptives like condoms are widely used, despite the strict anti-birth control views held by the Vatican.

Evangelical Protestants are the fastest growing religious group. Many young people from poor backgrounds have joined evangelical groups, seeking answers to their economic and personal problems. Worshippers lead a very strict lifestyle and go to church regularly. Church services are lively events, full of singing and chanting. In some services, followers speak in tongues (when they believe the Holy Spirit speaks through them), and priests perform faith healing ceremonies.

Another religious movement that influences many people's lives is Candômblé. This religion combines African rituals mixed with Catholicism and Amerindian customs. According to believers, everybody has one or two spirits known as *Orixás* that influence our personality and protect us through life. Only a Candômblé priest or priestess can identify somebody's *Orixá*, and during a Candômblé ceremony, many devotees offer gifts like special foods to their *Orixás*. Priests and priestesses chant and dance for many hours before they enter a trance. For believers, this marks the moment when they are possessed by an *Orixá*.

▼ The statue of Christ the Redeemer on the Corvocado, one of the steep hills in the heart of Rio.

The city as a magnet

In the last 40 years, most of Rio's immigrants have come from other parts of Brazil rather than overseas. The city is a magnet for thousands of families in the poorer regions of Brazil, especially the northeast. Many have poured into the city in search of a better job, health care, or a decent school for their children, but there is not enough land in Rio to adequately meet their housing needs.

Poorer families often have to find a place to live in one of the city's *favelas*. Today, there are more than 600 *favelas* scattered across the city with populations varying from a few dozen to hundreds of thousands of people. Rocinha is one of the oldest and biggest. It began in the 1940s when a group of squatters took over a hillside next to the rich downtown district of São Conrado. Since its early days

▼ The number of *favela* dwellers as a percentage of the total population.

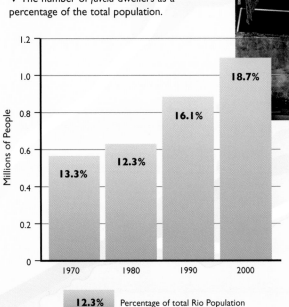

▲ Living in the favela means having to make the most of limited space, and often without much privacy.

Rocinha residents have displayed proactive citizenship in working together to make it a decent environment in which to live. With up to 250,000 residents, Rocinha is now a city within a city. It has its own schools, doctors' surgeries and fast food outlets.

Chart: Millions of People (y-axis, 0 to 1.2)

- 1970: 13.3%
- 1980: 12.3%
- 1990: 16.1%
- 2000: 18.7%

12.3% Percentage of total Rio Population

Maria Coetano, *favela* resident

Maria Coetano lives in Rocinha *favela*. She used to work as a dental receptionist in the city centre, but the pay wasn't good and she had to travel a long way to work

by bus. Now Maria has started her own business in Rocinha making special soaps. She has many kinds of soap for sale, using different fruits and spices to give each one a pleasant scent. Maria sells these to shops or directly to tourists who visit Rocinha on organised tours. Maria's life is much better now. She can walk to work, and she is making much more money than she did at the dentist's. Maria is now earning enough to pay for some of the fees of her husband's law course at night school.

Drug wars

Violence is commonplace in many *favelas*. On average, seven civilians and two police officers are murdered every week and after Johannesburg, South Africa, Rio is now the most violent city in the world. Most violence is linked to the illegal drug trade. For young *favela*-dwellers, drug-dealing is seen as a way to escape poverty – about 11,000 young men are now members of Rio's drug gangs, and half of them are under 18 years old. Since the introduction of crack cocaine, Rio's drug gangs have become armed, and even more dangerous.

They are powerful too – competing gangs control almost all the *favelas*. Battles between gangs have led to many deaths, and Rio's police operate a 'shoot to kill' policy when they raid a *favela*. As a result, the average life expectancy of a Rio gang member is only 29 years old.

▶ The high death rate among policemen make body armour essential.

Dangerous favelas

On March 31 2005, the city's worst massacre took place in Nova Iguaçu, a poor neighbourhood in the northwest. Thirty people were killed by a death squad, many of whom were off-duty police officers. Some people believe that it was a revenge killing for the arrest of other police officers accused of murder. The massacre was met with little reaction from people living in the *zona sul*. Many of them were preoccupied with mourning the death of Pope John Paul II at the time, and many regard violence in outlying districts as a distant problem that they would rather forget.

In the *zona sul*, Copacabana shares its name with the beach in front of this famous city neighbourhood. In the past, wealthy Portuguese plantation owners brought their families here for a weekend outing. Today, Copacabana has a huge mixture of people with different backgrounds and pay packets. At 25,000 people per square metre, it also has one of the highest population densities in the world. With space at a premium, rich residents live in high-rise apartment blocks that line the beachfront. Many of these apartments are now holiday homes for the very rich of São Paulo.

Safe suburbs

Other cariocas have chosen to move to the outlying suburbs. Today, more than 130,000 people live in Barra da Tijuca along the coast to the west. Nicknamed, the 'Brazilian California', families living here can bring up their children away from the noise, pollution and higher crime levels of downtown Rio. Barra da Tijuca has also become Rio's newest hub of Brazilian and overseas companies that are attracted by the safer, cleaner and less crowded environment.

Barra da Tijuca is Rio's youngest neighbourhood. Building only began 40

▼ Desirable high-rise housing in Copacabana apartment blocks on Avenida Atlantica, overlooking the bay.

▲ The shopping mall in Barra da Tijuca

years ago, and planners learned from the mistakes of other areas. Like an American city, Barra da Tijuca has wide avenues and roads, and large, spacious condominium complexes. The town also has South America's largest convention centre, called Riocentro. Residents have plenty to do thanks to a five-kilometre strip of shops and entertainment facilities. 'Barrashopping' is the largest shopping mall – with over 650 shops and apartments, offices, restaurants, cinemas, even its own monorail. Barra da Tijuca also boasts five theme parks and 21 nightclubs, and the beach is Rio's longest and cleanest stretch of sand. What's more, residents can still easily reach downtown Rio.

Living on the edge

Not everybody in Barra da Tijuca enjoys a luxurious lifestyle. New favelas like Jacarezinho (or 'little alligator') are springing up, home to the construction workers, maids, nannies and porters that work in Barra da Tijuca. Jacarezinho residents cannot afford the rents and house prices of the gated condominiums and have to make a home where they can. Unlike the favelas downtown that cling to the city hillsides, the flatter terrain keeps Jacarezinho out of sight. Most homes are without even basic services like piped

▲ Cramped housing in Jacarezinho – homes for the domestic help of Barra residents.

water, electricity and sewage disposal, making conditions here some of the very worst in Rio.

Home on the streets

The poorest residents have no house at all, and live on the streets. Many of them are children for whom the street is a work place to earn money supporting the rest of the family. Working days for these children are long, and home may be too far away, especially if they don't have the money for a bus fare. Many return home only at weekends, and spend the other nights sleeping rough. For others, the streets are their home, day and night. Many have run away from home because of a family breakdown, domestic violence or abuse. Others have no family at all. Street children have to make a living and fend for themselves, but life can be difficult and dangerous. Many are at great risk of catching sexually transmitted diseases as they are forced into prostitution to make money. Up to a quarter of street boys in Rio are encouraged to become 'soldiers' for a drug gang. Young recruits are nicknamed 'little planes' as they act as messengers between drug dealers and users, and some children as young as four years old carry weapons.

Children in danger

Caught up in the drugs war, Rio street children live in a more dangerous environment than many of the world's worst war-torn areas. Vigilante death squads have murdered some children. They see street children as a menace to be removed from the city's streets.

▼ Children sleeping rough on the streets of Rio where they have to look after each other.

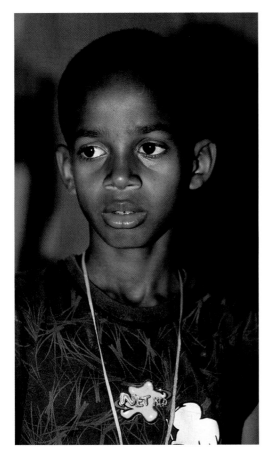
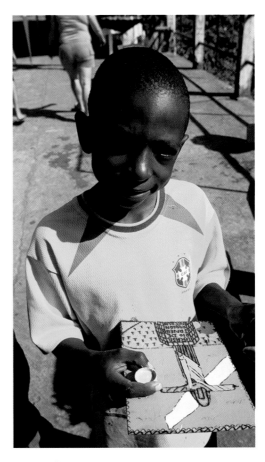

▲ Children may be made to work in many ways, including helping to sell tourist souvenirs.

Corrupt police officers sometimes join these death squads to top up their low salaries. When military police gunned down eight children sleeping on the steps of Candelària Cathedral in 1993, it made the headlines across the world. Although there have been no mass killings since the international outcry that followed, individual murders of children have continued. Amnesty International estimate that 90 per cent of these murders go unpunished.

Crusade for Minors

A number of organisations, supported by city residents, are giving Rio's street children a chance of a better life. The non-governmental organisation, Cruzada do Menor (or 'Crusade for Minors') has set up a special shelter in the Cidade de Deus housing project that caters for 70 young children. Here, children can get food and medical care, and Cruzada workers provide help for their families. Some of the support from Cruzada do Menor takes place right on the streets, where workers offer medical and dental treatment to children that have no family to which to return. Once a child builds trust with a Cruzada worker, he or she is taken to one of the organisation's shelters, where they can learn to read and write, or gain other skills in workshops to improve their chances of getting a decent, legal job in the city. One of the city football teams is even training some of them to become professional football players.

Living in the city

Rio was one of the first cities in the world to have a water supply system. From 1750, the Arcos da Lapa aqueduct channelled water from the Carioca River in the mountains to Rio's earliest inhabitants. Rio was also the fifth city in the world to have its own sewage treatment plant. But with the relentless urbanisation of the city, Rio's planners now face serious difficulties in providing these and many other vital services.

Services

Rio de Janeiro's water supply and sewage is operated by the Companhia Estadual de Aguas e Esgotos (CEDAE), a state company. Today, three quarters of the city is connected to the water mains, and the city's network of sewers is 6,900 kilometres long. To prevent pollution of the city's beaches, sewage is pumped several kilometres out to sea. But much of the sewage is not treated, especially the sewage generated by many favelas. Instead of soiling the beaches it fouls the seawater and creates more pollution elsewhere.

▲ A water main snakes down the hillside above Rocinha favela.

Leila Hizer

Leila Hizer works for the state water company, CEDAE. As a company, they have responsibility for providing clean water to the people of Rio. But today, the geography of the area and the growth of the city is making life difficult for Leila and her colleagues. The geography of the land was one of the reasons why people settled here in the first place. The steep mountains behind the city had many fresh water springs. With such a large population the city needs more and more water. There are no large rivers nearby so water is taken from the Paraiaba River a long distance away and then channelled in long pipes to the city's treatment plants. It is difficult to install the pipes through the mountains, and the steep descent into the city makes the water pressure very high by the time it reaches the city. A lot of the water from the Paraiaba River is already heavily polluted by industrial plants on its banks before it is extracted. Sewage treatment is another challenge for CEDAE.

A lot of people live close to the sea, which makes it difficult to find places to build treatment plants away from residential areas.

Living without basic services

Older favelas are linked to the city's electricity grid and water supply, and community organisations have organised their own waste disposal services. Others use illegal connections to the grid and mains known as 'gatos' to get their water and electricity. But provision of basic services is almost non-existent in the city's newest favelas. Here, there is no running water, and sewage runs down the side of makeshift streets. This puts more residents at risk of catching a water-borne disease like dysentery. Waste collection is another difficulty for the city authorities. Every two months, the city could fill the vast Maracanã Stadium with the amount of waste produced by city residents. Some favelas are regarded as 'no-go' areas, so there are no city waste collection services there at all. The uncollected waste blocks drains, increasing the risk of flooding, as well as presenting risks to health.

An end to smallpox

In the early 1900s, Rio was one of the most risky cities for catching a deadly disease like smallpox. In 1902, a young doctor, Oswaldo Cruz, was told to rid the city of the disease. To fight smallpox Oswaldo made it compulsory for every city resident to have a vaccination. Many locals were angry at being told what to do, and rioted in the streets, setting light to trams and buildings. Nevertheless, within months, smallpox in Rio had become a disease of the past.

D-Day against dengue

Today, residents have to be wary of dengue, a disease carried by mosquitoes that is difficult to treat. Dengue is sometimes known as 'break bone fever' as sufferers experience painful itching inside the bones and a high fever. Although the disease is rarely lethal, people sometimes have to take months off work or school to recover. More than half of all the dengue cases in Brazil are in Rio. Standing pools of water in streets, courtyards and potted plants after heavy rain provide perfect breeding grounds for dengue-carrying mosquitoes, and the disease can spread quickly in densely-populated areas. During the most serious outbreak in 2002, there were about 1,000 new cases in the city every day and 37 people died across Rio. Hospitals were at breaking point and the city authorities even threatened to cancel the annual Carnival. The 'D-Day against dengue' was launched to stop the spread of the disease. Over a thousand soldiers joined 700,000 volunteers to remove areas of standing water across the city, and to teach residents how to keep dengue mosquitoes out of their homes. More campaigns have followed since 2002, and so far, Rio's residents have avoided another dengue epidemic on this scale.

▼ Pools of standing water, like those in these gravel pits, are a home to dengue fever-carrying mosquitoes.

▲ Health organisations have joined with groups of residents to try to eradicate dengue fever.

An example to the world

Like many cities of the world, the growing numbers of people living with HIV/AIDS is a real concern in Rio. But thanks to a widespread education programme, cariocas are more aware of how to avoid infection. Condoms are now widely used after a campaign led by Rio's large gay community.

Brazilian companies copy drugs made by international companies and sell them at very low prices to help Brazilians living with HIV. In recognition of Brazil's success in tackling HIV/AIDS, Rio hosted an HIV/AIDS international conference in July 2005 for 6,000 health experts.

CASE STUDY

Dr. Daniel Becker, SEDAPS

Dr. Becker works for SEDAPS, to get better health care to the poorest areas of Rio. According to Dr. Becker, the health service in the city is very poor. There are state-run hospitals but a combination of corruption and poor organisation means that the care they provide is very basic. To get good health care, you have to pay. Dr Becker trains health care workers based in favelas to work more along the lines of health care in Cuba. The idea is to teach people how to avoid getting ill. Sometimes this involves education about purifying drinking water. Sometimes it means tackling the social problems that cause poor health, such as unwanted pregnancies and drug taking.

Primary school for all?

Compared to other parts of Brazil, Rio's children have a better chance of getting an education than most. The literacy rate for children above ten years old is 93 per cent, well above the national average. Rio is the only city in Brazil where every child between seven and 14 years old is guaranteed a free place in school. Thanks to 500 day care centres and 200 nurseries there is an effort to provide education for children under seven. But the statistics do not tell the whole story. For many children brought up in favelas, school is not an option. Some of them are too scared of drug gangs to go to schools near their homes. Others are already recruited by drug gangs before they are school age. As a result, there are still many children in the city that have no education and grow up without being able to read and write.

▼ School provision for seven to 14 year olds in Rio is the best in Brazil.

Dona Cidinha, youth project leader

Dona Cidinha works on a project to help young people that live in the district of Manguiera. In Manguiera, schools are open in two separate shifts, 7.30 am to 12.00 pm for one batch of children, and then 12.30 pm to 5 pm for another. This means that children are not at school for half of every day. The project provides a wide range of activities for their hours out of school. Dona and others on the project team teach children different skills that will be useful to them in later life, and help to keep them away from criminal activity. Thanks in part to the project, Manguiera has one of the lowest crime rates and highest numbers attending school of any district in Rio.

Further education

Those families that can afford to send their children to private secondary schools where the facilities can be as good as any in the world. State schools are free but many lack resources and equipment. Teachers' pay is very low too, and some schools struggle to find enough qualified staff.

Even though the city has a number of universities that students can attend for free, students from state schools struggle to get a place. To succeed, they have to pass tough entrance exams, but it tends to be the students from private schools that make the grade.

▲ Adult education classes offer the chance to make up for a missed education.

The Rio economy

After São Paulo, the state of Rio de Janeiro is Brazil's largest industrial powerhouse, and continues to have a fast rate of industrial growth. Situated in Brazil's richest region, 65 per cent of the country's trade, 40 per cent of its agricultural production and 70 per cent of the cargo transported through Brazil is within a 500 kilometre radius of the city. In Rio itself, there are well-established manufacturing industries in cars, petrochemicals, pharmaceuticals and shipbuilding.

▲ Petrochemicals form a large part of the city economy, and are an important employer.

Financial worries

Like the rest of Brazil, Rio's economy has suffered from periods of hyperinflation when prices have shot up overnight. Higher costs through inflation make it difficult for companies to do business, and customers never know how much more they will have to pay for goods in shops. Today, inflation is more stable, but the country has a very large overseas debt, and this will remain a burden for many years to come. Even though large amounts of money are raised from taxing people and businesses, most is spent on paying interest on debts to foreign banks, instead of being spent on improving the city's roads, hospitals, schools and other services. Some Rio residents argue that other money disappears into the pockets of corrupt city officials.

Attracting business

Despite its debt Brazil's modern economy is much more open to foreign investment, and many overseas companies have chosen to open factories in Rio. Glaxo-Welcome, Du Pont, Coca Cola, Michelin and Shell all have bases here. Car companies are keen to locate in Rio too. Both Volkswagen and Peugeot-Citroen have factories on the edge of the city to take advantage of the ready supply of steel from the CSN and Galvasud plants nearby. Companies in Rio also benefit from Brazil's membership to Mercosur, a trading bloc in South America that enables Rio-based companies to trade more easily with companies in other Mercosur countries. Through Mercosur, they have access to a market of more than 200 million people.

▲ International companies have set up in Rio, attracted by the natural resources and cheap labour.

Offshore reserves

Rio is also fortunate to have a plentiful supply of energy to fuel the city's industrial powerhouse, and the city is making plans to become self-sufficient in energy in the future. Half of Brazil's natural gas and 90 per cent of the country's oil supply are found in two basins offshore. Petrobras, Brazil's largest company, is in charge and the company is building six new natural gas plants to satisfy the city's energy needs. Rio is also the only city in Brazil to use nuclear power as part of its energy mix. There are already two nuclear power stations nearby and a third is being built.

▼ Natural gas storage facilities.

Services for the new century

Nearly three quarters of working people in Rio are employed in the service sector. The city is an important commercial and financial centre. Downtown in the financial district, modern skyscrapers sit next to some of the city's historical landmarks. BNDS, one of the country's most important investment banks, has its headquarters here along with the Bolsa de Valores do Brasil, Brazil's second biggest stock exchange.

Thanks to the large number of universities, research centres and three technology parks, Rio has become a centre of research and technology.

With 40 per cent of the country's IT industry based in Rio, the city is Brazil's nerve centre for telecommunications. IBM has its Brazilian headquarters here, and new fibre optic networks connect Brazil to the rest of the world.

▶ The move from a manufacturing-based economy to a services-based economy has led to the building of many modern tower blocks.

A multi-media centre

The media industry has also benefited from the boom in technology. Along with offices of some of Brazil's national newspapers, South America's biggest commercial TV network, called Globo TV network, is based in Rio. Globo is the fourth largest network in the world, and makes soap operas that are sold to many other countries. With its dramatic setting, the city is also a popular movie-making location, and a growing number of residents are employed in the movie industry as producers, camera operators or even as extras in front of the camera.

▲ Large tourist hotels back all the major beaches.

Tourism boom

With about 1.7 million tourists a year, tourism is another important mainstay of the economy. The city is Brazil's number one tourist destination with 40 per cent of all visitors to the country, and acts as a gateway to the rest of Brazil. New convention centres like Riocentro in Barra da Tijuca bring in international business delegates, and many hotels have been built around the bay to provide accommodation for holiday makers and business travellers all year round.

CASE STUDY

Francisco Rodriguez

Francisco Rodriguez is a waiter in a hotel in the district of Flamengo. He has been working in the same hotel for 15 years. Francisco is now one of the head waiters, and earns enough to support his wife and two children, and have a small house in one of the favelas near Flamenco.

Most of the guests in the hotel are on business trips to Rio. They stay in Flamenco because it is close to the city centre and has a much more relaxed atmosphere than more famous places like Copacabana – there are also fewer incidents of violent crime and guests feel safer at night.

Informal economy

For many people in Rio, the 'informal economy' (where no taxes are paid on income) is where they make their money. Without welfare support unemployment is not an option. Instead, people set up small businesses using their own skills. There are over 800,000 of these small businesses in the city either on a street pavement, or operating from family homes. Many believe that city services would collapse without the contribution of these independent entrepreneurs. The city government has recognised that these small enterprises have been able to absorb more than 200,000 workers that were made redundant from the formal economy.

Unlike normal jobs that follow office hours and have a pay cheque each month, jobs in the informal sector are much more flexible, depending on when and where there is a demand for their services. Sometimes services are paid in other goods rather than cash. Without official registration with the government, some informal businesses struggle to get bank loans, and few are insured against accidents

▼ Small businesses, like this fruit and vegetable stall, are common throughout the city.

at work. Almost 40 different kinds of documents from three levels of government are required to make one of these small businesses legal, but the city is working to reduce this bureaucracy. Over 400 computer centres have been opened since 1998 in order that informal workers can learn essential new computer skills. The city has also worked to convince the private sector to give 'micro-loans' to small entrepreneurs that work in the informal economy, allowing them to expand.

CASE STUDY

Oswaldo da Souza, walking salesman

Oswaldo da Souza is a walking salesman, or *àmbulante*. He sells blankets and shawls to people on the beaches of Copacabana and Ipanema. In 1984, Oswaldo and his family moved to Rio from north east Brazil. They used to live in the city of Fortaleza, but most of the land and businesses were owned by just a handful of rich families.

There was very little work and most of the jobs available were badly paid. When Oswaldo first moved to Rio, he worked as a porter in one of the hotels on Ipanema's seafront. Thanks to the tips from guests, he saved a little money.

In 2001 Oswaldo stopped being a porter and started selling things on the beach. He really enjoys this job – he can meet people from all over the world, and he has learned to speak a little English, Spanish, Italian and Japanese. He even earns more than he did as a porter. At night, Oswaldo returns to the favela where his family live. It's not far from the beach, and he has managed to build a small, comfortable house there.

Managing Rio

During the years of military dictatorship up to 1985, Rio was starved of economic investment as the generals saw the city as a political threat to their leadership. Since free elections began, following the removal of the military, Rio de Janeiro has had its own mayor. The mayor's office is responsible for the city's administration. One of the greatest issues facing the city's mayors has been giving the residents of Rio's *favelas* a voice, by ensuring that they are involved in the decision-making processes that affect them.

Rights for citizens

From 1988, a new constitution gave all Brazilians a guaranteed right to free speech, and 16-year-olds could vote for the first time. All citizens within the state of Rio de Janeiro can now vote for a governor every four years. The state of Rio has a legislative assembly that decides on levels of taxes and has its own judicial system. Within the city itself, people vote for a mayor every four years to run the city's affairs.

Cesar Maia has been re-elected three times as the city's mayor. Maia remains unpopular with some, but during his time in office, he has overseen important projects that have improved the lives of many of Rio's poorer citizens such as the Agentes da Liberdade ('agents of freedom') programme that helps to rehabilitate and reintroduce convicted criminals into society. The mayor abolished speed limits in high-crime areas in an attempt to stop car-jackings. He also started a policy called Remedio em Casa, which allows patients to receive prescription medicines by post.

To create Rio's entrepreneurs of the future, the city authorities also provide money and training for young people. This way, they can start their own businesses, and make more of a contribution to the city's economy.

▶ The headquarters of the the City Government of Rio de Janeiro.

The Favela-Bairro project

Other projects have focused on housing in the city. Unlike the military regime before them, today's city authorities are upgrading the *favelas* rather than pulling them down. In 1994, the Favela-Bairro project began to transform favelas with 500 to 2,500 households across 330 neighbourhoods into legal settlements with their own services like paved roads, sewage systems and waste disposal facilities. By consulting with the people who live there, 'Favela-Bairro' has a better chance of bringing more suitable and lasting improvements to the *favelas*. But after so many years of neglect, managing improvements in the favelas has proved difficult following the infiltration and growing power of drug gangs. Even the Favela Residents Associations, originally set up to air the views and needs of local people, are infiltrated by gang members. Nevertheless, Favela-Bairro remains the city's most important improvement project, and there are plans to invest another US $1 billion. Of the 1.7 million people in Rio's slums, 500,000 have benefited since its start.

▼ An important part of upgrading the *favelas* has been trying to improve the legal and economic position of the self-employed. Over 1.1 million cariocas are self-employed workers in the informal sector.

People power

Despite more than 15 years of democracy, many residents remain suspicious of politicians, and national corruption scandals have not helped. In one of the city's elections for a new mayor, the Brazilian Banana Party used a chimpanzee called Tião (big uncle) as their candidate. Under the slogan, 'vote monkey, get monkey', the party came third in the election with more than 400,000 votes, demonstrating just how disillusioned voters had become. Many people turn to citizens groups to voice their concerns instead. In Rocinha, the independent organisation Viva Rio has a website for residents called 'Viva Favela'. The website raises awareness among all cariocas about life in Rocinha and helps to dispel some of the stereotypes of people who live there. The website has a larger readership than many national newspapers. Set up in 1993, Viva Rio also acts as a link between the police and favela dwellers, and runs drop-in centres that offer free legal help, and counselling for victims of violence.

CASE STUDY

Daniella Broitman, journalist

Daniella Broitman lives in the district of Leblon and works as a journalist and film maker. Recently, she has been working with a few of the poorest favela communities in Rio. Some of the leaders of these communities wanted to attend the World Social Forum that happens every other year in Porto Alegre, southern Brazil. The World Social Forum is a conference of up to 100,000 activists from all over the world who gather to share ideas on how to lift people out of poverty. By taking part in the World Social Forum they hoped to highlight their belief that with better help and less corruption from the city authorities, the lives of favela dwellers could be so much better. Normally, people from the favelas wouldn't be able to go to the conference as they can't afford to get there. Daniella decided to raise money to cover their costs. In return, she made a documentary film about life in their communities, and their experience at the conference.

Improving the 'City of God'

Elsewhere in the city, projects to improve living conditions are run by non-governmental organisations. On Rio's western outskirts, a housing project called Cidade de Deus (or 'City of God'), home to 60,000 people, was the subject of an award-winning film in 2003 that described the true stories of young men who lived there. Cinema audiences worldwide were shocked by the scenes of poverty and violence in the 'City of God' movie, but many residents claim that the reality is even worse. Today, the NGOs Action Aid and CEACC (Research Centre for Cultural Action and Citizenship) are working together to improve life in Cidade de Deus. They are providing health education classes, sports and leisure activities for children, and are supporting a community radio station.

▲ Children from Cidade de Deus learn how to play musical instruments.

▼ Keeping children off the streets saves them from the attentions of drug gangs and helps them learn new skills.

Transport for Rio

Many years ago, people crossed the city of Rio in streetcars pulled by mules. With the introduction of electricity, a network of trams replaced the mules. Today there is only one tourist tramline left, and most people use buses or the subway system.

Clogged streets

Most people travel by bus or car along a network of roads that criss-cross the city. Some residents have to change buses many times to get to work. Two railroads transport another 100 million passengers a year between the city centre and the main suburban and rural settlements on the outskirts. There are too many vehicles clogging the streets of modern day Rio, and traffic congestion is a major problem. Journey times across the city get longer and longer, and during rush hour the air is choked with exhaust fumes.

Alternatives

To ease the traffic problems on the roads, a subway system was built to carry up to 250,000 passengers a day underground between its 21 stations. Travelling by the Metro is clean, safe and air-conditioned, and there are plans to extend the network to Ipanema and Barra da Tijuca.

Another way of reducing Rio's traffic problems is by encouraging people to leave their car at home and cycle to work instead. Since 1992, an 84 km network of bicycle lanes runs through most of the beachfront districts, and more lanes are being added to the industrial suburbs in the west.

◀ Too many cars on too little road space can lead to grid-lock during the rush hour.

▲ A dedicated bicycle lane. The lanes are used for leisure as well as commuting.

▲ The light railway and the subway provide a more sustainable and cleaner option than car travel.

Tunnels through the mountains

Rio's mountainous terrain creates a major headache for transport engineers. To link different parts of the city, they had to build 23 tunnels through the serra. In 1997, a new route called the 'Linha Amarela' (yellow line) opened that stretched 25 km from the international airport to Barra di Tijuca. Although drivers have to pay a toll to use the route, they can now avoid the traffic jams of the old city roads. Some commuters claim that journey times to work downtown have since halved. The 'Linha Amarela' is an impressive engineering achievement. In some places, the road had to be built on stilts to navigate round the steep cliffs overlooking the bay. Engineers also had to dig four gigantic tunnels through the mountains. The longest, called Covanca, is over two kilometres long.

◀ A tunnel on the Linha Amarela.

Sugar fuel

Many cars in Rio have been converted to run on both petrol and an alcohol made from sugar cane, which is produced in the areas around the city. Alcohol is cheaper by volume and less polluting, but the cars tend to be less powerful when run on alcohol. Many drivers switch to petrol to get up hill, and Rio is a very hilly city.

▶ Alcohol and ordinary petrol are both sold at the petrol stations of the big oil companies.

CASE STUDY

Joao Mendes, taxi driver

Joao Mendes lives in Copacabana. He is 67 years old and for more than 40 years he has driven one of the cabs in the city. Joao's taxi runs both petrol and alcohol. With a flick of a switch, Joao can change the fuel used. For taxi drivers like Joao, it is really difficult to drive around the city between 7 and 9 am in the morning and between 6 and 8 pm at night. Joao thinks the new tunnels have had little effect. It still takes him more than an hour and a half to drive the 25 km from the airport to Barra da Tijuca along the Linha Amarela. In fact, he thinks the traffic situation is just getting worse and worse.

Taking to the skies

Thanks to its modern airports Rio is the main hub for air transport in Brazil. Each year, 15 million passengers use the international airport that is named after one of Rio's most famous musicians, Antonia Carlos Jobim. The airport also boasts South America's most modern cargo terminal. Towards the heart of the city, land has been reclaimed from the sea to build Santos Dumont airport. It is only minutes from the city centre, and operates flights to many other parts of the country.

Crossing the bay

Traditionally boats have been used to cross the bay, including the hydrofoil below. The Niterói Bridge has made travel across Guanabara Bay easier. Stretching 14 km, the Niterói is the longest bridge in the world. Since it opened in 1975, drivers have used the bridge's six lane highway to cross the bay to reach the town of Niterói, instead of taking a 100 km trip around the bay's edge. Around 150,000 vehicles cross the bridge every day.

▼ Foot passengers can cross the bay by hydrofoil.

▲ Rio's airport is the busiest in Brazil.

▼ The Niterói Bridge is the longest in the world.

Culture, leisure and tourism

For cariocas, going to the beach is a way of life. Even after dark, residents enjoy the beautiful white sand stretching eight kilometres along the city's rim. At weekends, the beaches are particularly busy. Parasols and beach loungers are available for hire, and the beach is crammed with bronzed bodies. Even for the most dedicated sun-worshippers, parasols are a must on the hottest summer days. Storms and sea breezes bring some relief, but temperatures can still sometimes reach a scorching 40°C, making activity unappealing.

Local food and drink

Behind Copacabana beach on the Avenida Atlantica there are juice bars offering many drinks made from freshly squeezed fruit. Other bars sell caipirinha, Brazil's national drink. A glass of caipirinha is a mixture of cachaca, a strong alcohol made from distilled sugar cane, and crushed limes, sugar and ice. Others quench their thirst with a beer on tap served in a frosted glass, known as a *chopp*. There is a large beer brewing industry in the city. For food, restaurants known as *churrascarias* offer an 'all-you-can-eat' feast of delicious barbecued meats. Rio is also the birthplace of *feijoada*, Brazil's national dish. African slaves were the first to cook feijoada using scraps of pork thrown out by their owners. Today, feijoada is a stew made of pork, sausage and beef served with rice, slices of orange, and egg mixed with manioc flour.

Beach sports

For many people, the beach is also an important place for sports, socialising and even business. Between Copacabana and Ipanema, the waves at Arpoador provide good conditions for surfing. Elsewhere, the beaches are dotted with makeshift football pitches or volley ball nets where people can perfect their skills barefoot on the sand.

▼ Many beach sports are variations on the theme of football, including a form of volleyball where the players cannot use their hands. Competitors travel from around the world to compete on Rio's beaches.

Ancient arts on Sundays

On Sundays, the beach road is closed to traffic all the way from Leblon to Leme, and turns into a pedestrianised promenade for all sections of Rio society. In Ipanema, people practise *capoeira*, a kind of martial art that was once the pastime of African slaves that lived in Rio centuries before. To the sounds of drumbeats and a wooden, stringed instrument called a *berimbau*, *capoeiristas* form a circle and take it in turns to twist, turn and try high kicks in the air. Like an ancient form of breakdancing, the best *capoeiristas* are highly skilled in their moves.

▲ Few cities have good surfing right on their doorsteps. Sun, sea, and an exciting nightlife make Rio a haven for surfers.

CASE STUDY

Paulo Pires, surfer

Paulo Pires is a surfer. Of all the beaches in Rio, Paulo's favourite is the one at Barra da Tijuca. Here, Paulo thinks the water is much cleaner than elsewhere, the waves are good for surfing and he can meet other young surfers. The beach at Barra da Tijuca is so good that it will be used as one of the venues for the water sports competition when the Pan-American Games come to Rio de Janeiro in 2007.

Football rivalry

Like the rest of Brazil, people in Rio take their football very seriously, and many young cariocas dream of becoming the next football legend. Ronaldo, voted world player of the year and top goal scorer in the 2002 World Cup Finals, was born in Bento Ribeiro, a poor neighbourhood of Rio. Like other Brazilian football stars, Ronaldo has since moved to play in Europe, where he can earn a much bigger salary. Nevertheless, followers of the city's football clubs, Botafogo, Flamengo, Fluminense and Vasco, are passionate and rivalry between supporters is intense.

During the Copa Americá and the World Cup Finals, supporters of all local clubs join together to back the national team. During the 2002 World Cup, fans could watch Brazil play games at the cinema. When Brazil won the trophy for a record-breaking fifth time, overjoyed revellers filled the streets and partied for the whole day after.

About 15 km west of the city centre is the Nelson Piquet International Racing Circuit. Many residents are as fanatical about motor racing as they are about football. Every year, a Grand Prix race is held here. The area was once a large, marshy area dotted with lagoons, but the area was drained and new roads added, including the Avenida Ayrton Senna, named after one of Brazil's best ever Formula One drivers, who was killed in an accident in 1994.

Leisure at the lagoon

Another lagoon, called Lagoa Rodrigo de Freitas in the neighbourhood of Lagoa, has been developed into a leisure area right in the heart of the city. Surrounded by the richer neighbourhoods of Ipanema, Copacabana and Leblon, people spend an afternoon here boating on the water, or walking through the surrounding parkland. The more energetic can jog, cycle or roller blade round the 8.5 km pathway that circles the lagoon.

▼ Football is like a religion for the city's residents. The supporters of different clubs enjoy a passionate rivalry, but join together to support the national team whenever it plays.

Adventure tourism

Rio offers plenty of attractions for its visitors. As well as a tour of the city's centre and a visit to the beach, the cable car ride up Sugar Loaf mountain is on every tourist's itinerary. But new types of tourism are available where visitors can experience more adventurous activities. Keen hikers can go to Tijuca National Park or walk the long route up to the summit of Sugar Loaf mountain. The most adventurous can try hang gliding from one of the city's mountain tops, or even skydiving.

CASE STUDY

Paulo Eduardo

Paulo Eduardo works for a hang gliding tour company. Hang gliding is very popular here, especially amongst younger tourists, and there are now more than 16,000 flights a year from Pedra Blanca, a steep mountain in the city. It costs US$80 a flight, including a pilot who flies the hang glider alongside the beginner. The flight lasts ten minutes, and the views from the air are fantastic. Tourism is one of the biggest employers in Rio these days, and tens of thousands of people like Paulo would not have a job without the tourists that visit the city.

▼ An exciting way to see the city!

Carnival!

Some international visitors come just for Carnival, Rio's biggest party of the year. Carnival takes place before Lent in February and is an important event in every carioca's calendar. For four days, Rio's streets are crammed with people coming to see or take part in the colourful Carnival parades. All day and all night, people dance to the pulsing rhythms of samba, a musical style born in Rio.

There are many forms of samba. An informal jam session called *batucada* happens in local bars. People drink, sing and use a table to bang out a samba rhythm with their hands. Bossa nova (meaning 'new style') is a world-famous laid-back form of samba developed by Brazilians in the late 1950s. The bossa nova classic, *'A girl from Ipanema'* is the fifth most played song in the world. It was written in 1962 about a beautiful girl who often walked past the Bar Velosa in Ipanema.

Some people take most of the year to get ready for Carnival. Community groups in Rio's *favelas* have their own samba schools, with up to 6,000 members. Each school chooses its own costume theme and song to perform during Carnival. The competition between samba schools is intense – students have to practise for hours together to get their rhythm and dance moves exactly right. When Carnival finally arrives, up to 90,000 spectators pack into the purpose-built Sambódromo where the schools compete against each other to be voted the best of the year. They each have an hour to impress the judges, spectators, and millions of others watching the spectacle on television.

▲ This girl is training for her Carnival routine. Preparations begin months in advance.

▶ Samba dancers in costume, ready to perform in Carnival.

▲ The floats that take part in the Carnival parade can be huge, and jaw-droppingly extravagant.

Happy New Year!

New Year is another special time of celebration in Rio, particularly on Copacabana beach. Here, an old tradition taken from the Candômblé religion (see p. 17) takes place the night before New Year's Eve. Dressed in white and blue, Candômblé priestesses wade into the sea to throw flowers as a tribute to the sea goddess, Yemanja. On New Year's Eve itself, two million people – young, old, rich and poor – gather to enjoy free concerts on the beach, and dance barefoot on the sand. At the stroke of midnight, everybody goes into the sea to throw white flowers, and fantastic fireworks light up the sky.

The dress code for New Year's Eve follows tradition too. Everybody wears white for the party, but a flash of red is a sign that someone is looking for romance, yellow to wish for prosperity, or green to wish for good health.

The Rio environment

Environmental extremes are normal for Rio de Janeiro. Guanabara Bay suffers from serious pollution, and over a million people live among slums that have millions of tonnes of uncollected waste. Yet close to the city centre is a pristine urban forest, the largest in the world.

▲ Tijuca National Park may be a world away from the city centre, but it is easy to reach by public transport.

Emperor to the rescue

Fifteen minutes inland from the beach, people can escape the hustle and bustle of city life and explore the creeks, waterfalls and dramatic mountain scenery of Tijuca National Park, covering an area of 3,200 hectares. In the early 1800s, much of this area was cleared to grow more sugar cane and coffee. In the 1860s, Brazil's last Portuguese emperor, Pedro II, bought back the land from the plantation owners and started a huge replanting programme. Today, the park is the last patch of Atlantic Forest that once blanketed the area. Atlantic Forest is a special environment thanks to the moisture that rises up from

▲ Rare tamarind monkeys survive in the park.

the Atlantic Ocean and smothers the mountain slopes in a blanket of water vapour. Trees with carpets of mosses and ferns grow well in this damp, misty climate and the Atlantic Forest is rich in wildlife, including howler monkeys and giant otters.

Disaster strikes

Elsewhere, the Atlantic Forest has been cleared to build houses, grow crops or use the trees as timber. Destruction of the forest has led to disaster in Rio. Heavy storms in spring sometimes create deadly rivers of mud that mix with debris from illegal garbage dumps and sweep down the valleys. Without the trees to stop them, these mudslides cascade down the mountain slopes, engulfing everything in their path. In December 2001, 66 people died when their houses were buried in mud from one of these mudslides.

Erosion, flooding and mudslides remain a serious threat to the safety of people who inhabit the hillsides on Rio's outskirts.

But in the city district of Botafogo, the forest cover has been restored, thanks to the efforts of the Society for the Friends of Reforestation (FLORESCER), a non-governmental organisation. With the support of the local media, FLORESCER started a campaign in 1994 to explain to people living in Botafogo why the forest was important to their lives and to the environment. Since then, local people have joined volunteers from across the city to replant the mountain slopes with tree species. Central to the project were children in local schools. As well as planting new trees themselves, they have helped to spread the message about the importance of trees to their parents and neighbours. Today, the slopes above Botafogo are once again covered in forest, protecting the community from the risk of mudslides. Elsewhere in Rio, people have built crash barriers from old car tyres to halt the mudslides in their tracks. This way, they are recycling waste and protecting houses at the same time.

▼ Average temperatures and rainfall for Rio de Janeiro.

▼ Hillsides that have been cleared of trees are at greater risk of landslides after heavy rain.

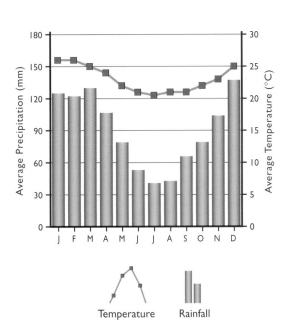

Pollution of Guanabara Bay

Pollution is a big problem in the vast Guanabara Bay next to the city. When the explorer Amerigo Vespucci and his crew first entered the bay on New Year's Day 1502, the waters were teeming with whales and dolphins in a rich marine environment. Today, much of the marine life is badly damaged. The whales and dolphins have long since vanished, and fishermen have watched their catches fall by 90 per cent. Pollution presents health risks to people too as waterborne diseases like typhoid have become more common in the bay area.

Guanabara Bay is polluted in many ways. Part of the problem comes from the 55 rivers and streams that flow out into the Bay. Many of them are contaminated with untreated sewage and waste from factories, hospitals and homes in the city. Meanwhile, the removal of most of the mangrove forests that once surrounded the bay has made the problem worse. These special forests used to act as natural filters, trapping dirty sediments and keeping the water clean, and also as nurseries for young fish.

Accidental spills of oil and heavy metals from tankers, pipelines and ports add to the problem. One of the worst occurred in 2000 when a pipeline burst at a Petrobras oil refinery, spilling about 1,300,000 litres of crude oil into the bay. To make matters worse, the bay is quite enclosed so the pollution tends to collect in the Bay rather than get dispersed in the open sea.

▲ Waste from homes and factories can go straight into the bay in many parts of Rio.

▲ ▶ Keeping the bay clean helps to promote the tourist industry, and fishermen can catch more and healthier fish.

The long clean up

In 1994, the Rio state authorities decided that drastic action was needed to clean up the bay. With help from the Inter-American Development Bank and the Japan Bank, US$1 billion was pledged to the Guanabara Bay Clean Up Programme. The first priority was to invest in more treatment plants to stop raw sewage from entering the bay. Some of the money was spent on building incinerators and recycling plants in the city so that less waste was dumped in the water, and in some areas, mangrove forests have been replanted to clean the water naturally. Since 2001, Petrobras has contributed to the clean-up effort. The company has spent over US$100 million on improving the safety procedures for its pipelines and refineries to prevent future accidents. Scientists guess that it could be another 15 years before the bay waters can be declared properly clean and safe again.

Cleaning up the city

Cariocas generate about 8,600 tonnes of waste a day, and some of it is just left littering the city's beaches. But a clean-up project called 'Praia Limpa' (clean beach) is encouraging beach-lovers to take responsibility for the mess they make. Run by a group of non-governmental organisations, 'Praia Limpa' is beginning to change people's bad habits. Today, locals and tourists can dump their rubbish in free waste sacks.

Recycling rubbish left on the beach and elsewhere in the city is becoming a new way of making money for some of Rio's poorer residents. These *catadores* comb the streets picking up aluminium cans and other waste and take it to recycling centres. Here, they are paid for the rubbish they collect. Other *catadores* work in the recycling centres, sorting and separating rubbish into different materials ready to be recycled. Today, there are about 3,000 *catadores* in Rio. Some of them can now earn enough from recycling to live in a decent home and support their families.

▲ Waste that is dumped in the sea will wash back onto the beach. The beaches need constant cleaning.

◄ Many poorer cariocas make their living by collecting recyclable waste.

▲ Sewers that drain into the bay need constant monitoring to ensure that it remains unpolluted.

A plan for the twenty-first century

Since 1992, people around the world have associated Rio with care and concern for the environment. In that year, the city hosted the world's first Earth Summit at the Riocentro conference centre in Barra de Tijuca. At the summit 122 world leaders gathered to discuss how people were damaging the environment, and to work out a plan of action to tackle these problems in the twenty-first century, known as 'Agenda 21'.

To put Agenda 21 into practice, each country agreed to draw up its own plan to involve local communities, businesses and schools in recognising what damage they do to the environment and to support them in developing more sustainable ways of living and working. In Rio itself, a team of people based in the city's universities have created a 'green map' of the city to make residents more aware of the value of the city's environment and to take action to protect it. The map highlights the importance of the city's public parks, and encourages people to support eco-tourism and recycling projects in the city. It gives advice to architects on how to design buildings that do less harm to the environment. The map also provides tips on how cariocas can stay healthy. For example, cycling routes are featured on the map to encourage more people to cycle rather than drive in the city.

The Rio of tomorrow

As Brazil's centre of technological innovation, Rio is well placed to remain an important global city of the future. By sharing new ideas with other scientists and engineers around the world, the creative thinkers in Rio's research centres and universities may invent new technologies that will improve the way we live in the future.

Brazil is already exchanging technologies with China, now the country's third biggest trading partner and the world's fastest growing economy. Both the Brazilian and Chinese governments are keen that this relationship becomes stronger in the future. Brazil has also joined forces with South Africa and India. Collectively known as the 'G-3', these three powerful developing countries are fighting together for a bigger share of world trade. A better deal in world trade would be a real help to the people that live in Rio's favelas. By getting a fairer price for the goods they make, more of them will get a chance to escape poverty. Technology will help too. As more favela residents learn how to use a computer and the internet, they can shop around online for the best prices for goods and can access a world-wide market for the things they make themselves.

The creativity of favela dwellers may bring new trends in music and culture to the world. Young people in the favelas have developed fusions of samba and hip-hop, and their brand of 'funk' that mixes drum and bass, techno and samba is becoming popular in European nightclubs.

▼ The city government will continue to invest in projects to improve the plight of the poorest cariocas.

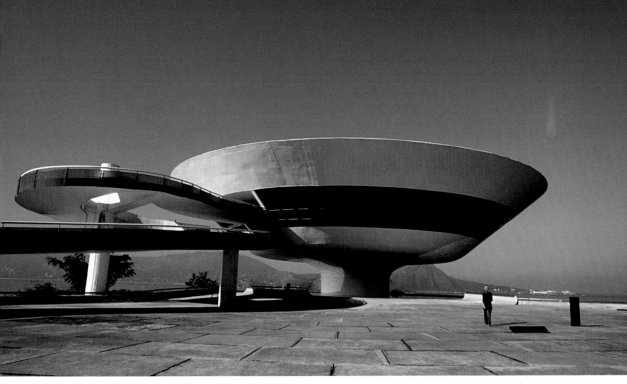

▲ This modernist building by the Rio architect Oscar Niemeyer expressed his hopes for the future of the city.

Host to the Americas

Many residents are excited by the forthcoming Pan-American Games that will be hosted by Rio in 2007. During the 16 days of the competition, Rio is expecting up to 500,000 extra guests. Preparation for the games is well under way. New facilities are being built, including a 'village' for the competitors in Barra da Tijuca and an extension of the Metro line out to the suburb. More than 50 years after it was first built, the Maracanã stadium is also getting a much needed make-over. Both preparation for the games and hosting the actual competitions will create thousands of jobs for cariocas. What's more, they will be able to use these new facilities long after the games are over.

Many residents of Rio are very positive about the future of the city, despite the many and pressing problems it faces.

▼ Today's children will face a future of rising urbanisation and environmental problems, but the city is planning and acting to solve those issues in a sustainable way.

Glossary

Amerindians Another term for American Indian.

Aqueduct A man-made channel for water.

Colony A territory ruled by an overseas state.

Coup A sudden violent or illegal seizure of power.

Dictator An absolute ruler who does not use or recognise a constitution.

Eco-tourism Tourism that does not harm the environment and respects local residents.

Erosion The wearing away of rocks and other deposits by natural or human action.

Evangelical Protestant Christian sects within Protestant Christianity that emphasise the authority of the Bible, and the importance of personal conversion.

Favela A Portugese word for a shanty town or slum.

Globalisation The process of opening up trade and financial markets to allow them to operate internationally.

HIV/AIDS Human Immunodeficiency Virus (HIV) is a virus spread through unprotected sex, contaminated needles or blood supplies. It can develop into Acquired Immuno-Deficiency Syndrome (AIDS), which is fatal. Expensive drugs can keep people alive, but there is no cure.

Informal Economy The unofficial economy dominated by small-scale and unregulated businesses or individuals that are not registered, deal in cash and rarely pay any taxes.

Legislative assembly An assembly of representatives of a city, state or country that meet to debate and vote on laws.

Lent The Christian period lasting 40 days from Ash Wednesday to Holy Saturday. It is usually a period of fasting.

Life expectancy How long someone might live.

Multicultural The presence of many racial groups, nationalities and cultures.

Non-Governmental Organisation (NGO) An organisation that acts in a proactive way according to its own agenda but is not tied to any national government.

Plantation A large farm generally producing one sort of crop, such as sugar cane.

Samba – A traditional Brazilian music.

SARS A highly contagious disease properly known as Severe Acute Respiratory Syndrome (SARS) that emerged in Asia in 2002 and spread quickly as people travelled around the world.

Service Industry (Sometimes called Tertiary Industry). Industries that provide services for people and companies such as taxis, banks and shops.

Suburbs The outer areas of a city where housing dominates.

Sustainability Living in a way that does not spoil the world for future generations, for example making sure that trees that are cut down are replaced.

Urbanisation The process by which a country's population becomes concentrated into towns and cities.

Vigilante An individual that takes the law into their own hands, often acting violently.

Further information

Useful websites

http://ipanema.com/ and www.explore-rio.com/ are two websites that give a local's overview of the city, with pages on Rio's food and nightlife, history, culture, sport facilities and top attractions.

Visit www.copacabana.info/historical-places-in-brazil.html for lots of information about the Copacabana district of Rio. The site includes maps, stories and images.

www.favelafaces.org/ uses video interviews and images of four people that live in Rio's favelas. The website really helps to explain what it is like to live in a favela, and the problems the residents face.

For information and images of Rocinha, Rio's oldest and biggest favela, visit www.rocinhaproject.com/facts.html

To find out more about Rio's Carnival, visit www.carnaval.com/cityguides/brazil/rio/riocarn.htm. The site also features pages on samba and Rio's samba schools.

To find out about adventure tourism activities available in Rio and see some amazing images, visit www.riohiking.com.br/

Books

World in Focus: Brazil Simon Scoones (Hodder Wayland, 2006)

The Changing Face of Brazil Edward Parker (Hodder Wayland, 2004)

Countries of the World: Brazil Brian Dicks (Evans, 2005)

Rio de Janeiro Regis St Louis (Lonely Planet Guides, 2004)

Carnival in Rio Helmut Teissl (Abbeville Press, 2000). Photographs from Rio's annul celebration.

Useful addresses
Embassy of Brazil
32 Green Street
London WIK 7AT
Tel : 020 7399 9000
www.brazil.org.uk

Index